DR. GOLIATH

by David Steele

Illustrated by Marshall Potter

HIRAM
DICKENS
PRESS

P.O. Box 11724, Pittsburgh, Pennsylvania 15228

To the people of Christ Presbyterian Church
Who daily encourage a pastor
More adept at doggerel
Than dogmatics.

Hiram Dickens Press
Post Office Box 11724
Pittsburgh, PA 15228

Library of Congress Catalog Number 87-072593
ISBN 0-9619538-0-2

Manufactured in the United States of America
1   2   3   4   5   6   7   8   9   10

My growing-up church did not believe boys and girls
should share the same curriculum. So, from the time
I could read until I began to shave, I was a member
of the BOYS' CLASS. Mr. Stumm was our perennial teacher.

Mr. Stumm shunned teachers' guides and lesson plans.
He taught Bible stories. He knew them all
and told them with enthusiasm. Week after week
we listened to Mr. Stumm's Bible stories . . .
year after year. We must have heard them all.

Mr. Stumm was not concerned with relevance
or moral teaching. So far as I can recall,
we did not discuss the stories. We did not seek
to pull from them eternal truths.
Mr. Stumm was interested in one thing:
He was going to get those stories into our heads.
He succeeded.

I suspect Mr. Stumm trusted God would show each of us
just what the stories meant. He was right.
Through the years, in high times and in low,
a story comes to my mind. A story with insight,
once about someone in the Bible . . . now about me.

I often say a silent prayer of thanks for Mr. Stumm
and his Bible stories, for I have learned that many,
many people never met a Mr. Stumm and have grown up
unaware of the great and small stories in the Bible.

It is a handicap; for above all the Bible
is the grand story of God's reaching out toward
human beings. We are meant to notice the congruence
between the stories of our own lives and God's great
story. But how can we, unless we know the stories.

So these poems came to be. Sometimes they are
about the Bible . . . a retelling of the Bible in terms
we can understand. Sometimes the verse begins with
something that happened to me and moves into the Bible.
Always there is movement from God's story to our own
and back.

The poems are meant to be fun, though their subject
is often very serious. They are lighthearted
but, I trust, not lightheaded. Fun, but they do not
make fun of the Bible, nor do they think the Bible
is funny. Fun, because God has a sense of humor.
Humor can be a means of grace. We often see God's truth
more clearly with a twinkle in the eye.

I urge readers to check the Bible passage
as you read the poem. If you enjoy the verse,
read it to a friend. Joy like faith is meant
to be shared.

Perhaps these stories will remind you
of one of your own. Tell it to a friend.
It is a mystic moment when human beings tell
and listen to the simple tales that are
of the essence of life.

David Steele
San Rafael, California

Contents

Dr. Goliath

I Samuel 17:1-11, 38-50

Dr. Goliath, B.A., D.D.
Was humanity raised to the Nth degree
As he smiled benignly atop his perch
In the lofty pulpit of Old First Church.
He spoke of faith with firm conviction,
With dulcet tones and perfect diction
Till I, and all within that place,
Were lifted to the throne of Grace.

The skepticism I had borne
All week was gone on Sunday morn,
For then I'd see that Doctor G
Was never plagued by doubts like me.
How he preached the Word of God!
My friends and I were overawed;
His words of faith renewed, restored
Our contact with the Living Lord.

Often he'd be asked to pray
At Rotary or PTA.
With depth and feeling Dr. G
Brought God to our community.
And no mere teacher could surpass
The power of his Bible class,
For in his presence we all knew
That God was real and faith was true.

So, every weekly day of rest
We felt ourselves at peace and blessed.
We praised our gracious Lord and Master
For sending us this godly pastor.
And then one day in February,
He ran off with his secretary!
A Frog! That was my holy Prince!
(I haven't been to worship since.)

In The Beginning

Genesis 1:1

I read, "In the beginning, God . . ."
What gives my heart this gentle prod,
And turns my thoughts to life anew?
I wonder, Lord, might it be You?

I'm rather skilled in life's great game.
My moves, long grooved, remain the same.
Gone are the errors and the fears
Which plagued my early rookie years.
I've played with skill (and had the breaks).
So why, right now, for heaven sakes,
Should I be thinking of "beginnings"
Here, within these middle innings?

My life is good. I'm not aware
Of brooding thoughts or dark despair.
I'm rather sure I'd be content
To spend my days as they've been spent.
Why do I hanker to begin
Now, when my hair is getting thin?
Can some fresh vision form and rise
Before these long bi-focaled eyes?

Lord, I'm no kid of five or six.
I doubt if I can learn new tricks.
Yet, I've the inner feeling You
Are nudging me toward something new.

Well, Lord, I guess this silly grin
Implies I'm ready to begin!

The Spies

Numbers 13:25-33

Opportunity, they say,
Approaches every door,
Knocks once before she goes away,
And then is seen no more.
Oh, I wish that I were wiser,
For seldom do I recognize her.

My eyes are rather weak,
And I simply can't be certain
That she's the one I seek
As I squint behind the curtain.
So, everytime, the little lass is
Gone before I find my glasses.

Upon the edge of Palestine
Camped Moses and his band.
Those yonder fields, by God's design,
Would be their Promised Land.
They wondered in that desert quiet
Had they the strength to occupy it?

Moses chose twelve faithful men
To be his nation's spies.
"Infiltrate the border, then
Become our ears and eyes.
Report to us if you can see
The shape of Opportunity."

Forty days the spies were gone;
The time was far from short.
When they at last returned, at dawn,
They rendered this report:
"The soil is rich . . . the weather sunny.
It is a Land of Milk and Honey."

"Yet, this land we dearly prized,
We cannot take at all.
The people there are oversized,
And we are much too small.
They're giants . . . fearful, awesome thugs
Who'll squash us like so many bugs!"

But Caleb rather disagreed;
He was a different sort.
And so he raised his voice to plead
A minority report:
"We'll take this land without much fuss;
The people there are just like us."

He wasn't heard, of course,
Though his manner was defiant,
For no one will endorse
Going up against a giant.
To follow him might risk defeat;
The people knew when they were beat.

They later learned those spies
Had thrown a wicked curve.
Fear had clouded up their eyes
And destroyed their optic nerve.
But Israel acted on their fears,
Turned back, and wandered forty years.

I understand those spies
When I must make a decision.
With astigmatic eyes,
Can I be a Saint with Vision?
   Oh, knocking Opportunity,
   An Ogre you appear to me!

The Spies

Matthias

Acts 1:21-26

What happened to Matthias
Is not especially clear.
What caused this very pious
Gentleman to disappear?

He is introduced in Acts
At a moment of success.
We'd like to have more facts,
But he had a lousy press.

He had supped at Jesus' table;
He had been the Master's friend.
He was the sort of able
Soul on whom we all depend.

We know he was respected,
Had a spirit kind and docile.
He was the very first elected
To the office of Apostle.

He was honored by his peers
To receive a new vocation,
And he spent productive years
Doing church administration.

Yet, after his election,
Scripture grants him ne'er a mention.
Should not one of such affection
Be devoted more attention?

What happened to Matthias?
I have an answer that
May reveal my inner bias . . .
He became a bureaucrat!

He had no exciting capers,
For there's nothing much to shout
About a man who shuffles papers
From the In box to the Out.

We surely call the stabler
Folk to lead the church . . . and yet,
The name of an Enabler
Is quite easy to forget.

Matthias

17

Peter's Shadow

Acts 5:15

I noticed my shadow the other day;
And the child within who used to play
Kick-the-Can and Capture-the-Flag
Recalled the excitement of Shadow-Tag.

Shadow-Tag was my favorite!
"Step on your shadow . . . then you're it."
Such a scramble! I'll not forget
Maneuvering my silhouette.

Shadows, you know, are rather neat.
They stay connected to your feet,
Appearing docile . . . yet are known
To have ideas of their very own.

Many a time have I been tagged
When my body zigged and my shadow zagged.
How hard I worked to discipline
The antics of my prostrate twin.

Most children's games have one grand feature:
They serve us as a painless teacher.
That shadow gave me quite a sense
Of people and their influence.

I saw my shadow moving much
Beyond my range of reach and touch;
And thus I came to be aware
That though I'm here . . . I'm also there.

Of all the many stirring facts
Which Luke recorded in the Acts,
I've thought most often of the one
Brief scene of Peter in the sun.

You may recall the episode.
Peter walked along the road,
His thoughts much too preoccupied
To note the shadow by his side.

By that road, the sick had come
(At least the more adventuresome),
Simple folk who now were guessing
His shadow might bestow a blessing.

They reached toward him from couch and bed,
That his shade might touch the hand . . . the head,
Trusting that their convalescence
Might be speeded by his presence.

Maybe Peter never knew
About his shadow's rendezvous.
It's hard, of course, to realize
How we appear in others' eyes.

I'm sure he would have felt it tragic.
This trust in superstitious magic
Neither he nor God approved.
And yet . . . I bet . . . that he was moved!

To know your life has an effect,
That others view you with respect,
May agitate our human pride;
But, gosh, does it feel good inside!

There's much in life that we can fake
But not the shapes our shadows take.
We're summoned by the Holy One
To stand with Peter near the Son.

Peter's Shadow

20

Second Isaiah

Isaiah 40-66

Let us begin with a Biblical quiz:
What do you think of the Second Is.?
He is the one you may recognize
Is often referred to as Deutero-Is.
Do you think, as I, what a terrible shame
That we have no idea of this poor fellow's name?
Any author who takes all the pains which he took
Surely deserves his name on the book.

To people in darkness, he spoke of his sight
Of a future which sparkled with hope and delight.
He was, of the prophets, most keenly observant
Of all that's implied in the Suffering Servant.
His insights concerning both folks and events
Are a brilliant collection of uncommon sense.
What a shame that his writings, so pregnant with soul,
Were stuffed at the end of the Isaiah scroll
In Chapters Forty through Sixty-Six!
(That's one of life's most dirty tricks!)

(Of course, we all must realize
That some of this is Trito-Is.
Deutero must share his glory,
But that is quite another story.)

So many insights do we owe
This genius we call Deutero,
The chap deserves abundant fame!
At least, we ought to know his name.

He served his Lord without complaint.
I'm strengthened by this unknown saint
Who teaches me I'd best ignore
The things I don't get credit for.

Inverse Hypocrisy

Luke 18:9-14

Have you noticed how people who favor Christianity
    and democracy,
So often suffer from the symptoms of Inverse Hyprocrisy?
At least, the up-to-date Christians
    among my acquaintantship
Consider this variety of -ocrisy very hyp.

Now, the normal sort of hypocrite is quite easy to spot.
He brags a lot
And is quick to avow
She is holier than thou.
And while you listen to his vivid description
    of self-sanctification,
You are wise to keep one hand on your wallet
    and the other on your reputation.
Enough said! I need be no more analytical;
Of this sort we all are hypo-critical.

But the phenomenon of which I originally spoke
Tends to happen to somewhat nicer folk.
I am referring to the brand of hypocrisy I call "Inverse,"
Which is where a person instead of pretending that she
    is better than everyone else . . . claims to be worse!
It is as though God is having a contest to determine
    the world's most magnificent sinner.
And the inverse hypocrite desperately wishes to be
    proclaimed the winner.
So, to make a deep and abiding impression upon the judges,
She attempts to make a coal-black soul out of a few
  harmless smudges.

I know a goodly number of pleasant people who are
    considerate and lawful,
Yet spend much of their time and energy telling themselves,
    God, and me that they are simply awful!
They are the type who affirms
Those hymns about worms.

I have a hunch that this passion to appear vermicular
May be traced to one Biblical passage in particular.
I refer, of course, to the Gospel of Luke,
    especially that sector
Where Jesus discusses the praying Pharisee
    and the tax collector.
He reports that while the Pharisee prayed in pear-shaped
    sanctimonious tones . . . the publican's voice
    was quavering and thinner.
He could only manage to murmur, "God be merciful to me,
    a sinner!"
And while this prayer could not match the Pharisee's
    in content, style, or form,
It touched God's heart and made it warm.

Now, nowhere in this story does it appear
That the publican kept praying this same prayer
    year after year.
Yet, some have concluded that this means the surest route
    to impress God and win a heavenly crown,
Is to put themselves down.
And so they take to embellishing their rather
    mundane experiences until they come up
    with a semi-squalid story
Which proves they are worthless . . . and gives,
    they say, God the glory.
Just how God gets glory in all this
    is rather difficult to figure.

Inverse Hypocrisy

23

It assumes that if someone scrunches down
  and makes himself very, very small . . .
  then God gets bigger!
Actually this "miserable-worm" business
  becomes sooner or later
An insult both to wormdom and our Creator.
No worm I ever encountered spent time beating his breast
  and crying a mournful sob.
He was much too busy doing his job!

Worms display, as do most of God's creatures,
  a marvelous sense of dedication
Toward fulfilling their purpose in the great mystery
  of creation.
So, I fail to see any virtue which may accrue
From proclaiming that, while Yahweh did a superb job
  with the universe, God botched it in creating you.
So fie on anyone be she sincere or a faker
Who puts herself down and thereby degrades her Maker.

Now, I realize that we have all been carefully taught
Not to think of ourselves more highly than we ought.
But let us also confess
We will not think less,
For hypocrisy in any form is surely a curse,
And that includes inverse!

Inverse Hypocrisy

25

The Temptations

Matthew 4:1-11

I.

Then Jesus was led up by the Spirit into the
wilderness to be tempted by the devil. And
He fasted forty days and forty nights, and
afterward He was hungry. And the tempter came
and said to Him, "If you are the Son of God,
command these stones to become loaves of bread."
But He answered, "It is written,
  'Man shall not live by bread alone
  but by every word that proceeds
  from the mouth of God.'"

Jesus, I'm reading from Matthew's Good News
And trying to picture myself in your shoes.
(Or would that be sandals?) I know it's presumptuous,
For I've recently dined in a manner quite scrumptious;
And the passage on which I'm projecting my gaze
Begins with your fasting for forty long days.
I know I'm presuming . . . no colleague of mine
Has ever suggested that I am divine.
Oh, I'm ever so human, familiar with sin,
Yet, still . . . I would like to get into your skin.

I'm trying to sense how that fellow in red
Began painting those pictures inside of your head.
You knew right away that the tempter was near.
But, from my point of view, it just isn't that clear.

You refused to use faith to turn stones into bread.
Now, of course, I have read what the scholars have said:
This means you decided, you won't get a bunch
Of discerning disciples by serving free lunch!

26

But now, I dig deeper. Just where does this lead?
Are you telling me God is not there for my need?
As I look at myself . . . and at most of my friends,
It appears God's a means toward fulfilling our ends.
I mean . . . we want happiness, good health, and love,
So we turn in our prayers to the Great God above.

Well, your turning from bread is now giving me pause.
I sense Yahweh, for you, was no vast Santa Claus,
That the Lord God Almighty was really your friend
And that you would not use God as means to some end.
Do you think in my vigorous yearning for pelf
I can learn to know God as an end in itself?
'Cause all of my life, I must tell you, dear brother,
I've heard God is the answer . . . for something or other.
And I've come to expect in my affluent greed
That God really enjoys taking care of my need.

But now you suggest I adore God as God!
I'll give it a try . . . but that's terribly odd!

II.

Then the devil took Him to the holy city
and Set Him on the pinnacle of the temple
and said to Him, "If you are the Son of
God, throw yourself down; for it is written,
*   'He will give his angels charge of you,' and*
*   'On their hands they will bear you up,*
*   lest you strike your foot against a stone.'"*
Jesus said to him, "Again it is written,
*   'You shall not tempt the Lord, your God.'"*

Still here, Jesus, reading from Matthew's Good News,
Still trying to picture myself in your shoes.
I'm pondering how to discover just why
You turned down that marvelous offer to fly.

The Temptations

Oh, it wouldn't have worked in providing a source
Of committed disciples. I see that, of course,
For the folks that your soaring attracted were bound
To be seeking more thrills when you settled to ground.
But why'd you refuse, on that teetering shelf,
The feeling that leap would have given yourself?

I mean . . . people I know . . . say my good friends and I
Fervently want God to grant us some "high."
And if I stood with you on that towering butte
Quite convinced if I leaped, a divine parachute
Would sustain me; I'd jump. And I'd chortle with glee
For gravity's law is repealed, just for me!
But as you turned aside on that high temple ceiling,
Why, you just walked away from a fantastic feeling
Of God's undergirding. 'Twould see you through doubt.
And, tell me, aren't feelings what faith's all about?
But . . . you don't agree. It is less than appealing
This thought that your God might be good for some feeling.
And so you turned away. For in leaping you'd tend
To be quite involved in just using your friend.

I'm beginning to see faith, a bit, through your eyes.
Can I learn to love God, without seeking fresh "highs?"

III.

Again the devil took Him to a very high
mountain and showed Him all the kingdoms of
the world and the glory of them; and he said
to Him, "All these I will give you, if you
will fall down and worship me." Then Jesus
said to him, "Be gone, Satan! for it is written,
'You shall worship the Lord, your
God, and Him only shall you serve.'"

The Temptations

I see the third picture that fellow in red
Was painting that day on the screen in your head.
And I tell you straight out . . . and I hope you'll excuse,
But my culture won't let me get into your shoes.
For as I comprehend your approach on that tower,
You decided that day to shuck secular power.
It was yours for the taking. But there you were swerving
Toward something uncomfortable . . . something called serving.
Of servants today we are quite unimpressed,
They're patsies, or doormats, among the oppressed!

You see, I'm convinced that the down and the out
Will only improve by developing clout.
And I tend to believe that those people are blest
Who assertiveness train or develop in est.
Jesus, the question we're facing this hour
Is how people oppressed may gain access to power.
You stood on that hill, on that turbulent day
With it there in your hands! Why did you turn away?

I can't answer that question. Must I be more observant;
Note how you lived out your uniqueness as servant?
You spoke of the meek, and yet you were not weak.
I suspect in this fact is the answer I seek.

For insight I pray. For I would be that leaven
That brings into being the Kingdom of Heaven.

The Temptations

Og's Bed

Deuteronomy 3:1-11

On many occasions we've raised a dispute
Re: the spiritual value of Num., Josh., and Deut.,
Sections of which we find truly absurd,
Esp. accounts of the folk who were massacred
In the conquest of this, that, or the other village . . .
The amount of the plunder . . . extent of the pillage.
These bloody statistics of each armed patrol
Are hardly the rations which nourish the soul.

Yet, I have developed a strange fascination
With the tale of the war in the country of Bashan.
In the passage describing the death of King Og,
The author includes a unique epilogue.
He describes in great detail the size of Og's bed.
It measured 4 cubits by 9, so it's said.
"His bed was 6 feet by 13 and one half."
That is the gist of the king's epitaph.

What caused that old scribe to consider it vital
To pause in the midst of a bloody recital
Of the raped and the wounded, the maimed, and the dead,
With the story of Og and his wonderful bed?

I like to imagine the author was trying
To make the passage more bedifying.

The Good Samaritan

Luke 10:25-37

A dad makes a fuss
When he goes on a trip.
He packs up his bags
At a very fast clip.
He checks out the plumbing,
The car, and the lawn
And hopes nothing much
Will go wrong while he's gone.
He makes sure his wife
Knows the bills that need paying
And gives her the phone
Number where he'll be staying.
He calls in the children
At one time or other
To say, "I hope you
Will be good to your Mother!"
The children agree;
They smile and look pleasant,
For on his return
He may bring them a present.

Yes, when dads start to travel
They make quite a fuss,
At least in the families
That live around us.
And the fuss is the same,
If you wanted to measure,
When moms start to traveling
For business or pleasure.

With a dad leaving home,
Now our story begins.
He is saying goodbye
To his wife and the twins.
Each one gets a kiss
Then a hug or a squeeze.
As he walks out the door
His wife cautions, "Please
Be careful of robbers,
For I hear that they
Have been seen on the road
That you're taking today."
"Now, dear, don't you fret,"
He replies in a hurry.
"I'll be perfectly safe.
I don't want you to worry
Take care of each other;
I'll miss you, but you'll
See me next week."
And he climbs on his mule.
With a wave he sets off
At a pretty fast clip,
Glad to be started
On his business trip.

Now, this dad didn't show
That inside he felt funny,
For you see he was taking
A great deal of money;
And he had to admit
That his wife was quite right.
The road was not safe,
Especially at night.
But since he was going
To travel by day,
He didn't think trouble
Was coming his way.

The Good Samaritan

33

All morning he traveled.
It seemed safe enough,
For no one he passed
Looked especially tough.
And as he was thinking
Of stopping for lunch,
All of a sudden
A rough looking bunch
Of robbers surrounded
Our traveling dad.
They slugged him and mugged him
And stole all he had.
They took all his money,
His luggage, and mule.
He lay by the road
And he thought, "I'm a fool!
I shouldn't have traveled
Alone. Why, I knew
Better — Now, just
What am I going to do?
I'm in real trouble!"
And when he had spoken,
He noticed his ankle
Was twisted and broken.

He could just barely move;
And he started to hurt,
As he lay there alongside
The road in the dirt.
He lay there a couple
Of hours, at least,
When along that hot road
Came a fast walking Priest.
"I'm saved," thought our hero,
"I'm rescued at last!"
But the Priest didn't stop;

The Good Samaritan

He went hurrying past.
"My, good man, you've been
In a terrible crime.
I would like to assist you
But haven't the time;
And while I deplore
Leaving you in the lurch,
I must hurry on
To a meeting at church.
We're reading a number
Of very fine books
That tell what to do
For the victims of crooks."

"I'm already late;
It starts about noon.
I'm sure someone else
Will be coming by soon,
And I trust they will help
Straighten out your affairs.
So, farewell, my good man,
You will be in my prayers."

Off scurried the Priest.
You could tell he was busy.
Our dad lay alone
And began to feel dizzy.
He hoped some kind person
Would soon happen by
'Cause there in that desert
A fellow could die.

Well, before long, another
Traveler showed
Up by the side
Of that hot desert road.

The Good Samaritan

He stopped, and he looked
At our dad on the ground.
And he thought, "I suspect
There are robbers around;
And if I stop to give
This poor man some first aid,
Those bandits will get me
As well, I'm afraid."

So, he didn't stop either.
He simply called, "Peace!
When I get into town,
I will call the police.
I'm sure they'll send someone
To help you," he said.
"That's nice," thought our dad,
"But by then I'll be dead."

Time passed — It was nearly
The end of the day
When our dad saw another
Man coming his way.
"Oh no," he remarked,
"I can tell by his face
This man belongs to
The Samaritan race.
And all of my life
I've received this advice:
'Samaritan people
Are not very nice.'
They're dumb and they're meaner
Than most other folks.
And that's why we tell
Those Samaritan jokes.
I'm sure that the chances
Are awfully slim
That I will get any
Assistance from him."

The Good Samaritan

He couldn't have been
Any wronger, of course.
That Samaritan fellow
Got down from his horse,
He pulled out his canteen.
As quick as a wink,
Gave that thirsty father
A lovely cold drink.
Then cleaned off the blood,
All the grime and the dirt,
And splinted his ankle
So it wouldn't hurt,
Then carried our dad
To the nearest hotel
When he could relax
And begin to get well.

So soon our dad lay
In a nice, comfy bed.
When he was tucked in,
The Samaritan said,
"Good luck to you, friend,
I must be on my way.
The doctor will come by
To see you today.
You've had a rough time,
But you're still pretty strong.
I'm sure you'll feel better
Before very long.
I know you were robbed.
So when I go I will
Leave enough money
To pay up your bill."

The Good Samaritan

And he did! Well, you know
It is really a shame,
But our dad never learned
That Samaritan's name.
And when he got well,
He remarked to his wife,
"I can't even thank him
For saving my life.
I'd send him a note
If I knew his address.
But I may never see him again,
So I guess
I can show I am grateful
By trying to labor
To treat everybody I meet
As my neighbor.
For even a stranger
Can act like a friend."
And that brings this story
Of ours to THE END.

The Good Samaritan

The Jesus Fish

Matthew 28:16-20

Twelve bright fish swim up and down
The surface of my pulpit gown;
And once a year, I, as a rule,
Speak with the children of our school
Of how within God's grand design
The fish became a Christian sign.

Of early times we then converse,
When faith could lead to jail — or worse . . .
When Christian folks were strong and tough
And prone to cloak and dagger stuff.
They understand such folk would need
A special, secret shorthand creed.

And then before we say goodbye,
We count the fish — those kids and I —
The green, the yellow, red . . . we probe
The number on that fishy robe;
and our result is just colossal,
Twelve fish! That's one for each apostle!

There's Peter's fish, and this is James',
And so we go through all the names.
The children see my robe intends
To honor Jesus' special friends.
But then I pull a little trick
And question their arithmetic.

"You counted very carefully,
But there's a fish you didn't see."
There's one more there across my chest
Not appliqued like all the rest,
Just stitched with thread (I know that they
Can't see it from so far away).

And then I say, "Now, if you wish
We'll call this one the Jesus fish."
I tell the little guys and gals
What Jesus promised all His pals:
"Where-ere you go, what-ere you do,
I will always be with you."

Then those children chat with me
'Bout how to solve this mystery.
We see no arms, no hands, no head;
But Christ is here — that's what he said.
And then they start to realize
You can't see Jesus with your eyes.

"He's kinda like that Jesus fish."
(I think that's rather cleverish.)
And then I make a noble start
To show just how the human heart
Appropriates the Christly presence
(But that's beyond pre-adolescents).

Of Jesus fish those lads and lasses
Talk as they return to classes.
And I assume with confidence
That thoughts of Godly imminence
Growing from that piscine talk
Dance through the heads of my young flock.

Or so I thought. I now believe
I may have been a mite naive,
For now the story has been told
About that funny five-year old
And the field trip he took the week
He heard the mighty Chaplain speak.

The Jesus Fish

His class, it seems, had fin'lly come
To visit the aquarium.
And while his friends with happy squeals
Went off to watch the bass and seals,
He stood enthralled and stared point blank
Into an empty water tank.

His teacher wondered just what joy
An empty tank held for that boy.
As she approached, he whispered, "Shhish!
I'm trying to spot this Jesus fish.
If I keep still, perhaps he'll show,
They're quite invisible, you know."

Now, you would s'pose that wise adults
Could speak with kids and get results,
But what they hear inside the head
Isn't always what you've said.
The one who claims that he can tell
May lie 'bout other things as well.

The Jesus Fish

The Captured Ark

I Samuel 4:1-11

I seldom get into a fight,
But when I do . . . I know I'm right
And feel the Lord of heaven would
Assist me if God understood
The issues and the atmosphere.
And so I pray . . . to make them clear.

And that's the way the story goes
For human beings, I suppose.
At least, I see it very well
Within the Book of Samuel.

The Hebrews had this reputation
Of being God's annointed nation.
They were chosen and consigned
To be a light for humankind.
Well, you can see how they assumed
This meant their enemies were doomed.
They'd count on God to intervene
'Gainst Canaanite or Philistine,
And felt they had a guarantee
That God would bring them victory.

So, when the Hebrews fought this war
Of which we read in Samuel 4,
They knew the armies of those regions
Would melt before God's loyal legions.
But that day on the battleground
The Israelites were pushed around
By Philistines . . . well, you can bet
Those Godly folk were quite upset!

"What's happened to the Lord of Host?
Distracted? When we need God most?
We're getting licked! But now we find
There're other matters on God's mind."

And so with the avowed intention
Of getting some Divine attention,
Those Hebrews pulled a clever stunt.
They brought the Ark up to the front.

(Not Noah's Ark . . . the one that's meant
Is the Ark of the Covenant . . .
That sacred chest whose very essence
Symbolized the Holy Presence.)

Now having brought that sacred shrine
Of God up to the battle line,
The Hebrews knew without a doubt
They'd put the enemy to rout.
(It helps an army's self-esteem
To know that God is on their team.)

But there beneath those desert skies
The people found a strange surprise.
That enemy refused to yield
An inch of barren battlefield;
And ere long on that fateful day,
The Hebrews fled in disarray.
And then to add a further woe,
The Ark was captured by their foe.

Now, surely every saint or sinner
Supposes God will back the winner.
So, this is quite disturbing news:
That God would let those Chosen lose.
And, I suppose, we really ought
To give this matter further thought.

The Captured Ark

For it appears, we all assume
In battlefield or locker room,
The Lord has made a sacred pledge
To give God's team the fighting edge.
And, so, we find most everywhere
That every fight begins with prayer.

But God, we learn, does not begin
To root for pious teams to win.
For those the Lord decides to choose
Will sometimes win . . . and sometimes lose.
So it appears that God is not
As thrilled with winning as we thought.

God may refuse to aid our strife
To teach us Yahweh's view of life:
The purpose of the human race
Is more than first or second place.

The Captured Ark

The Other Nine

Luke 17:11-19

About that group of leprous men,
I get to thinking now and then.
Ten of them were in that band
Who felt the Master's healing hand.

Yet, only one within their ranks
Returned to offer Christ his thanks.
While his response was mighty fine,
What happened to the other nine?

How could those folk have been so rude
And fail to show their gratitude?
In microcosm here, we find
The thoughtless tale of humankind.

We live our lives at such a pace
We haven't time to ponder grace.
So I shall schedule in my days
Some time for thoughts of grateful praise.

But not today! I feel my oats,
I haven't time for thank-you notes.
So God who loves more than I ask
Is taking on a thankless task.

Oakland Coliseum

(An event at a ball game that reminded me of Acts 2.)

SUNDAY AFTERNOON SELL OUT.
We sigh with relief
As the two elderly ones
Carefully make their way
To the seats in front of us.
They are small, thin, and somewhat frail.
Our view will not be blocked.

In my mind, I name the one
Billy Martin's mother.
She places her cane safely beneath the seat,
Adjusts her baseball cap,
Plunks down the cushion,
And prepares herself for the work ahead.
Her chum is ageless.
I think, Abner Doubleday's sister.
She pats her freshly coiffed hair,
Puffs on her Marlboro,
And quotes statistics in a whisky baritone.
These two are no strangers
To Section 130 (Row 29).
This is their turf!

BATTER UP!
The young man inches his way
Through the crowded row
Toward the empty seat beside me,
Balancing a tray of eats and drinks.
He stumbles; loses control;
And liquid galore showers on the heads
Of the two oldtimers below.
He is embarrassed; mumbles an apology;
And scurries quickly to his seat.

But our senior citizens
Are not about to let this young whippersnapper
(Probably a Yankee rooter)
Get off without a verbal drubbing.
The air is blue with their comments!
These two did not pick up that vocabulary
In Miss Fine's finishing school.
"Seventeen hairdresser bucks shot to hell!
And *you* are sorry?"

TOP OF THE FIRST:
It is unseasonably chilly
In Section 130 (Rows 29 and 30).
The ladies up front discuss the
Unwelcome invasion of their turf,
While their humiliated assailant
Whispers to his wife:
"What do the old broads want . . . blood?"
We, and the other witnesses 'round about,
Find it difficult to concentrate upon the game.
Was that Winfield who just struck out?

3 UP, 3 DOWN:
Between innings, Billy Martin's Mother
Reaches in the pocket of her sweater
And chortles with delight.
She turns 'round to her beleaguered attacker,
Holding a piece of melting ice.
"I believe this belongs to you."

He takes it from her outstretched hand.
"Thanks, lady! Believe me, from now on
I intend to keep my possessions to myself.
It won't happen again."

Oakland Coliseum

"Of course, it won't honey," she says,
Smiles and pats his knee
With grandmotherly affection.
Abner Doubleday's sister nods approval.
The young man breathes a great sigh of relief,
As do we all.

The sun has broken through in Section 130.
We relax and bask in its warmth.
The flag in center field ripples in the breeze,
Blown, we are certain,
By the Wind of the Spirit.

Krazy George beats his drum.
We are ready now for the task ahead:
LET'S GO A'S.

Oakland Coliseum

Lord! Lord!

Matthew 7:21

Some Christians make me quite aware
Of their DEVOTION, FAITH, and PRAYER.

While other people seem to lead
Their lives involved in human need.

I've noticed that I tend, quite oddly,
To find the latter much more Godly.

The Wisdom of Solomon

1 Kings 3:1-28

King David ruled with spear and bow
Yet sensed that blood had had its day.
   He had in mind
   His son could find
A better way.

King David, mighty man-of-war,
Now yearned for violence to cease,
   So "Solomon"
   He named his son.
(And that means "peace.")

King David planned most carefully
Before his son assumed the throne,
   School for his pal
   More general
Than was his own.

King David, commandant-in-chief,
Excused young Sol from R.O.T.C.
   In peaceful mood
   The boy pursued
An arts degree.

When Solomon at last was king,
He had no interest in the sword,
   Another care
   He raised in prayer
Before the Lord.

King Solomon asked God to bless
(As he took on that royal guise)
  His mind, his head.
  Here's what he said,
"Please make me wise!"

Now, wisdom is a fitting quest
For anyone who serves or reigns.
  We do expect
  Folk we elect
Might have some brains.

War weary subjects praised this king
Increasingly as time went on.
  He found the root
  Of each dispute
With brains, not brawn.

Two women each had birthed a babe,
But one child perished in the night.
  Each claimed as son
  The living one.
Now who was right?

The king was asked to judge this case.
He pondered . . . then addressed his staff:
  "The answer's clear.
  Use this sword here,
And give each, half."

One woman smirked in victory,
The other blanched and pleaded: "Give
  The child to her
  For I prefer
That it should live."

The Wisdom of Solomon

And now a simpleton could tell
Which woman was the rightful mom.
　　Oh, what a thing
　　To have a king
With such aplomb!

So people praised the Lord by day
And thanked their God most every night.
　　God had ordained
　　A king to reign
Who was so bright.

So, Solomon ruled forty years
In splendor, pomp, and opulence.
　　His style of court
　　We must report
Caused great expense.

He had a first-class temple built
While sparing no expenditure
　　And raised the dough,
　　As you may know
Among the poor.

Those people rose in deep revolt
And overthrew that wise king's heir,
　　For he had spawned
　　A tax beyond
What they could bear.

So, Solomon was bright, all right,
He ushered wisdom into fashion.
　　Yet now we find
　　His brilliant mind
Lacked compassion.

When Jesus taught His special friends,
He did not speak of having smarts.
　　He hoped that they
　　Would pray each day
For loving hearts.

The Wisdom of Solomon

Ode To A Trinitarian Retirement

Matthew 6:28

(On the occasion of the retirement of John Hadsell, Ted Stein, and Margaret Veneman from the faculty of San Francisco Theological Seminary.)

"Consider the lilies of the field
Which toil not, neither do they spin."

Now there's a verse that fails to yield
Great meaning for John Calvin's kin.
We find Paul's insight much more neat:
"If you don't work, then you don't eat!"

Ogden Nash said:
   "So far as I know, mankind is the only
   section of creation
   That is doomed to either pers-
   or ex-piration."

Not "doomed," Ogden, it's how we oughter;
Brow sweat is our holy water.

So now we honor years well spent
In honest toil, within this place;
Yet wonder if retirement
Can ever buy a state of grace.
We dare not finally commend
A life where you'll not toil nor spin;
Such idleness we fear will tend
To place you in the jaws of sin.

So next year, Maggie, Ted, and John,
Should we meet—say at Safeway's door,
We hope you will rant on and on
'Bout how you're busier than before.

Don't show your tan — don't joke or laugh,
Or share with us disgusting facts
Of how you love just goofing off
And learned, at last, how to relax.

Dear friends, consider not the lily—
If not for your sake—then for ours.
Confirm our hunch that Christ got silly
While gazing at those stupid flowers.

Go labor on—spin till you bleed.
In honest toil confirm our creed:
That heaven's gates have never yet
Op'ed to a brow sans heavy sweat.

Ode to a Trinitarian Retirement

The Book

(An event that seemed, for a time, like the road to Damascus.)

Each Sunday school or seminary
(While technique is bound to vary)
Adjusts its course to guarantee
Grads with Bible lit'racy.
Each student learns, quick as a whistle,
To state the theme of Paul's epistle,
To give each verse a sound critique
Be it in Hebrew, English, Greek—
For Christians, it has been decided—
Daily, by THE BOOK are guided.

And surely this has proved the rule
Though not the way one learns in school.
No Christian worth her salt dares look
At days ahead without THE BOOK
In hand, before her eyes,
To guide, direct, prioritize.
But, alas, THE BOOK is liable
Not to be the ancient Bible.
THE HOLY BOOK, I must relate
We live by, is the one called "date."

For nowadays divine anointment
Ordains one to the next appointment.

In date books, be they old or new,
Are listed things we've said we'd do,
Meetings, classes . . . when and where . . .
Weddings, parties . . . all are there;
And usually there's space within
For phone numbers of kith and kin.

THE BOOK'S our life; that's why we start
To carry it above the heart.
'Tis precious; there's no doubt about it.
We dare not leave our homes without it.

So, with this prelude now resolved,
You'll sense, I think, how quite involved,
How far from ecstasy, elation
In New York City's vast bus station,
Was I that day I lost my breath;
Experienced fate far worse than death,
Dialed a number . . . left alone,
Forgot my date book near the phone . . .
Remembered, hastened back anon
To find my HOLY BOOK was gone!

Gone . . . GONE . . . G O N E ! ! !

Gone were the meetings, next month and this week.
Gone were the places I was scheduled to speak.
Gone was it all—it was nigh universal.
Gone all the weddings and every rehearsal.
Gone were the quotes that I hoped to remember.
Gone was the conference . . . was that in September?
Gone was the birthday of my lovely wife.
Gone were the touchstones which govern my life.
Gone was my future! dissolved in thin air.
Gone my identity!! Oh, such despair!

What sort of a fiend, how demented a crook
Would stoop to such depths as purloining THE BOOK.
I pictured his slavering jowls in my mind
As he thumbed through THE BOOK . . . I was not very kind
And I called hellish fire—unendurable fates
Upon that vile person who dares to steal dates
From another—and searched for a perfectly prime
Sort of punishment fit for this crime.

The Book

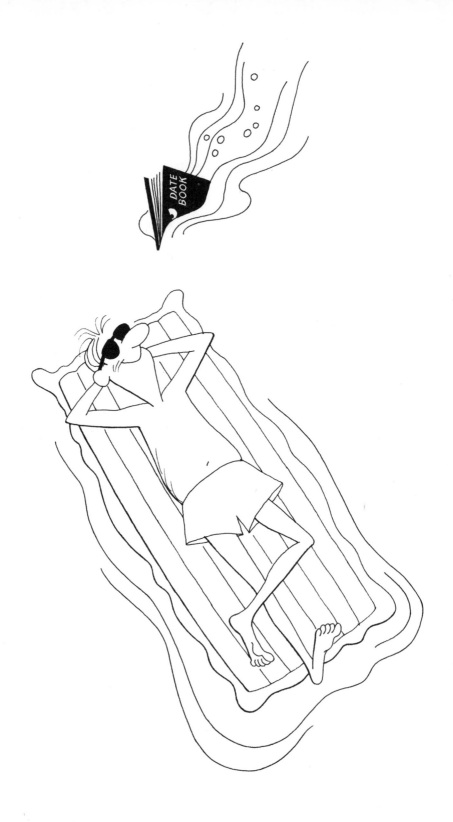

He might, as a start, as a way of hell's greeting,
Be compelled to sit through a 15-hour meeting.

"VENGEANCE IS MINE," saith the Lord.
Oh yeah! Not if I get there first!

Then something happened to assuage
My anger, calming down my rage . . .
Breaking through my inner shrillness
A voice, like the sound of a gentle stillness,
A voice from beyond, clothed in mystery
Whispered a message, "My son, you are free.
You've been granted a summer, a spring, and a fall
With nary a single commitment at all."
What an event! I had reached a stage
Where my life stretched ahead as a vast empty page.

And I thought then,
"I'm born again!
Why even look
For that stupid book!"

'Tis bliss to be alive and free,
With no responsibility;
To realize, say on next Tues-
Day I can do just what I choose.
Or should I wish some afternoon
Say, in the balmy month of June,
To see a ball game, get a tan,
No problem . . . why, of course, I can.
I might learn Chinese, or write a book,
Or give the Holy Land a look.
Like Adam I have each new day
To use as I choose—'most any old way.

WOW!

The Book

So I bask in the bliss, as you figure I might.
It endures through a day on a cross-country flight
And a night where the smile on my face fairly beams
As I peacefully enter the sweetest of dreams.
And I notice next morning on leaving from home,
I am gently enfolded in lovely Shalom.
But . . . on ent'ring the office, I'm given this greeting,
"We hope you remember that afternoon meeting.
Virginia would like to know how long you'll speak,
'Cause she's planning the stewardship dinner next week."

It hits me . . . when
I'm born again,
I better act fast,
'Cause it ain't gonna last.

And so began a busy day.
We can't throw boomerangs away.
Try as we might to be a loner,
Commitments sail back to their owner.
The garden's gone—as says the Word;
It's guarded by a flaming sword.
We're not permitted Sir (Or Madam)
The innocence of gentle Adam.

So how about lunch—doesn't that sound great?
Let me get out THE BOOK to be sure of the date.

The Book

The Web

(An event from my days as a school chaplain.)

Several times each week I grapple
With squirming kids in Thurston Chapel.
I ask: Can hearts be warmed and stirred,
Can children grasp God's Holy Word,
When words do not convey as much
As objects they can see or touch?
And so I search—yea—even sleuth
For ways that youth can see the truth.

The early symbol of the fish
Does all a man like me could wish.
It speaks of times when life was raw,
When Christian lived beyond the law,
And folks of faith were quick and nimble.
And so I use that piscine symbol
To lead the thoughts of my young brood
Into a Christly attitude.

Some days I find my flock is apt
To give attention less than rapt.
So, as I spoke, one day, of Glory
In language rather piscatory,
I did not feel inclined to mention
That I had sensed the kids' attention
Had wandered from the words I said
To something far above my head.

Now, speakers do not relish finding
Out their spell is less than binding:
'Tis difficult to sermonize
When one can see four hundred eyes
Watching something more appealing
Than you—upon the chapel ceiling.

65

And so with faltering conviction
I hurried through the benediction.
With heavy heart, filled with contrition
I tried to spot my competition.
And, sure enough, high in the air
Within an empty sky-light square
A spider swaying fro and to
Had formed his own construction crew.
Those kids had watched his swinging dance.
Of course, I never had a chance!

I noticed then that little guy's
Constructed right before our eyes
With actions rather feverish
A webby picture of a fish.
Is that a fish? Can that be true?
I moved 'round for a better view.
A fish it was! All new and glistening;
At last, I thought, someone's been listening!

With happy cries filled with elation
Caused by that spidery creation,
I summoned all the chapel crew
To share with them that wondrous view.
Was that a fish within that thread,
Or was it merely in my head?
They saw it too! Why, I declare,
That silky fish was really there!

I'm not inclined to make a fuss
Regarding the miraculous.
An engineer would, I should guess,
Describe in terms of force and stress

The Web

Just why that spider chose to drape.
His silk in that aquatic shape.
I don't suppose that creature meant
To conjure up a grand event.

Yet, at that time, within that place
His web became a sign of grace.
I wanted the whole school to see
This work of serendipity
And felt this arachnidan art
Would bring a lift to every heart.
For after all, it is my role
To share the things that feed the soul.

So, of that fish I planned to speak
At chapel services next week.
I asked my colleagues whether they
Had heard about some special spray,
Glue perhaps, maybe cement,
To make that picture permanent.
Oh, I thought, if I could choose
I'd bronze it, like my baby shoes.

Now, well-laid plans of men and mice
Eventually are imprecise.
So we neglected to address
Our thinking to the janitress.
She saw that web; her heart was vexed.
(Of course, you know what happened next.)
A pole, a rag . . . and swipe . . . our mystery
Passed into the realm of history.

Our fish was gone! You might infer
We'd be upset . . . of course, we were!
But then we saw this tale was tending
To reach a nearly perfect ending.

The Web

The circumstances made us face
The fact we can't hold on to grace.
God grants to us his gifts each day,
And then they simply fade away.

Manna made a tasty bite
But spoiled if hoarded overnight;
And rainbows leave us open-eyed
But surely can't be petrified.
So good gifts come—a spider fish,
A singing bird . . . a fulfilled wish . . .
And then they go . . . not to our sorrow;
Something else comes by tomorrow!

Who knows, tonight, within this place
We may be gently touched by grace.
The moment comes . . . we feel its glow
And just as gently, let it go.

The Web

The Fire Did It!

Exodus 32:1-24

When Moses had ideas for sharin',
He used to call on brother Aaron
Whose voice had timbre, depth, and reach
(The kind that makes an awesome speech).
Oft Aaron spoke the anecdote
Or the bon mot that Moses wrote.
With pear-shaped tones he'd eulogize,
And people gasped! and thought him wise.

The gift of gab can insulate
The public from one's mental weight.
Thus, Aaron's golden eloquence
Disguised his lack of common sense.
To hear him speak you'd ne'er suspect
That he was shy of intellect.
So few knew he was ill-equipped
For leadership—without his script.

Now, few of us can really see
The foibles of our family.
We give our kin—both clod and lout—
The benefit of every doubt.
And so it seems quite obvious
That Moses acted just like us
In giving Aaron leadership
When he went on that business trip.

Only a fool would dare to toss
Aside a summons from the boss.
When Moses heard God's call on high,
He packed his bags for Sinai

And left his brother in command.
We may assume that Moses planned
That surely he and God could do
Their business in a day or two.

And for a time things went quite well
Among those folk of Israel
Aaron's empty, vapid chatter
Didn't really seem to matter.
But then when Moses was delayed,
The group began to feel afraid.
"He should be back by now," they said,
"Something's wrong—He must be dead."

The days went by—their panic grew.
Poor Aaron wondered what to do
He didn't need a Gallup Poll
To sense that he had lost control.
When leadership has been defective,
A circus often proves effective.
So he suggested to his staff
That they construct a golden calf.

The populace was duly told
To bring their rings of shiny gold,
And there amidst those desert sands
They watched the skillful idol hands
Create a bovine deity
With agile spontaneity.
That work of awesome inspiration
Called for a pagan celebration.

They cheered and sang, broke into dance
And chug-a-lugged intoxicants
And joined in rituals, coed.
(The details best are left unsaid.)

The Fire Did It

And at that moment, staid and stern,
Moses made his grand return.
Down the mount, across the gorge, he
Stamped into that frightful orgy.

A group that feels prophetic fury
Can sober up in quite a hurry.
No one cared to laugh or joke.
They hung their heads as Moses spoke.
"You folks will go down to your graves
With the mentality of slaves.
How can I get you all to see
That only God can set you free?"

Now, leadership was far from bland
Whenever Moses took command.
He seized that calf and ground it up,
Mixed it with water in a cup,
And made them drink. "To what extent
Does this god give you nourishment?
Ask yourselves that crucial question
As you endure the indigestion!"

Not even Midas, we are told,
Enjoyed a meal that turned to gold,
And those folks felt a trifle crummy
With all that glitter in their tummy.
Indulgence wanes—Repentance gains
When one is gripped by gastric pains.
So Moses ended the affair—'n
Then looked up his brother Aaron.

"Aaron, I can't understand
How you let things get out of hand.
I've worked with you—I thought you knew
What God and I have tried to do.

The Fire Did It

73

But when I leave for several days
You lead them back to pagan ways.
I can't see how you could begin
To get involved in such a sin!"

Aaron thinks—and then produces
One of history's great excuses:
"Those restless ones were growing bold,
And so I had them bring the gold.
We heated it, and in half
An hour there appeared this calf!
It was created by the flame.
You see—I'm not at all to blame!"

So Aaron says—In each event,
We're pawns of our environment.
We each walk with steady gait
The path determined by our fate,
So, those who settle for his view
Are not at fault for what they do.
They simply follow their desire
And blame the product on the fire!

The Fire Did It

Recycling

Habakkuk 2:20

Some basic rules define the source
Of pleasant social intercourse:
When friends share cookies (chip or date)
We don't return an empty plate
But send it back all nicely spread
With slices of zucchini bread.
And piques of proper social training
Remind us, as we're entertaining,
To see that we do not forget
The people owed a dinner debt.
So, social bonds are smooth and flat
When glued with careful tit for tat.

But when it comes to heaven's grace,
Our tit for tat seems out of place.
How few of us command the wealth
To pay God back for kids or health,
For love, or comfort, friends and talents . . .
Our ledger's wholly out of balance.
We can't pay back the Lord above
For all God's countless gifts of love.

God's love comes to us as a trust;
And when we understand, we must
Find someone else by dusk or dawn
Who needs that love and pass it on.

The Lord is in the temple—enter
Into God's recycling center.

The Boy Who Said, "No"

Matthew 21:28-31

The dad addressed Son Number One,
"There's so much work that must be done
To cultivate and till our land,
Today I need another hand."

"Father, had you any doubt
That I'd be glad to help you out?
I absolutely guarantee
This morning you can count on me!"

"How fine it is to know my brood
Is positive in attitude."
So mused the loving father who
Now approached Son Number Two.

"Good morning, Son, today I find
My work has gotten way behind.
I'm wondering if you would stay
Beside me in the fields today?"

The younger boy seemed unimpressed
And unmoved by his dad's request.
He set his jaw and shook his head.
"Don't count on me!" was all he said.

Our troubled father tried to hide
The turbulence he felt inside.
"Some day," he thought, "I'd like to know
Why that boy always answers 'No'."

"We've had (myself and my good wife)
A positive approach to life.
Why, then, does our offspring give
The accent on the negative?"

Tears don't help when milk is spilt.
So bearing his parental guilt
(Which he kept pretty well concealed),
The father moved into the field.

The work had barely just begun
When who shows up?—his second son!
The boy who just awhile ago
Had spoken that decisive "No!"

"Hi, Dad, can you still use my aid?
Let's just forget my brief tirade.
I'd planned to be with friends today,
But you need help much more than they.

All day amidst that growing crop
The son worked right beside his pop
Who needed him; because, you know,
His older brother didn't show.

His reasons? Well, we'll have to guess.
It does appear his easy "Yes"
Did not commit himself to action.
So he fell prey to some distraction.

In this tale, Jesus bids us heed
The gap betwixt the word and deed,
Suggesting that commitment's essence
Is seldom easy acquiescence.

For oft a person really dares
To answer "No!" because she cares,
And then we find when we begin
To do the job, she pitches in.

The Boy Who Said "No"

And folk who give a facile "Yes"
Can leave a project in a mess,
for they're the type of volunteer
Who has been known to disappear.

So Jesus drew for our reaction
This picture of the Saint in action.
His portraiture so clearly shows
The ayes are not above the noes.

The Boy Who Said "No"

Where Were The Men?

Matthew 27:55-56

Good Friday is surely a sordid affair.
The soloist asked me today, "Were you there?"
So I made a deliberate effort of will
To position myself by that Golgotha hill.
I felt so ill-at-ease; and since violence tends
To upset me, I looked 'round to find Jesus' friends.
I could see, as I stood by that gnarled gallows tree,
That the crowd was not large as I thought it might be.
And as I looked it over, it dawned on me then
That the women were present. But where were the men?

Where were the men? From my Biblical classes,
I knew Jesus preached now and then to the masses;
But most of His ministry lived, ate, and spoke
With a rather small number of intimate folk.
And right off the bat they could see He intends
To develop a loving communion of friends.
They knew His compassion. You'd think they'd stampede
To find room near the cross with their friend in His need.
Their absence is puzzling. I ask it again:
Oh, the women were present; but, where were the men?

John made an appearance, at least for awhile;
But the absence of others I can't reconcile
With the fact that they loved Him. Why wouldn't you try
To be close to your friend on the day He must die?
I remember that night when He asked them to keep
Careful watch while He prayed. They had fallen asleep.
Do you think on that Friday when Jesus found harm
That His friends had neglected to set the alarm?
When the women reported the tears they had wept
Did the men say, "Oh, golly, we just overslept!"

80

Perhaps it is flippant to treat them this way.
The men could have been in a meeting all day,
Working like fury . . . with no coffee break!
Discussing appropriate action to take.
They may have condemned pagan Rome's persecution
And spread on the record a strong resolution.
Or . . . maybe those men were just quite at a loss,
'Cause the women departed to go to that cross
Leaving the males to decide what they would.
But with no secretary, a man's not much good.

I suspect that those men simply were not prepared
For a rigged execution. I suspect they were scared!
And when they checked the action, they probably knew
There was nothing at all for a fellow to do
But stand helplessly by and allow Christ to die.
Now what's to be gained if they give that a try?
Look . . . a group of strong men, slim and trim, and athletic
Wringing hands? Shedding tears? That would be so pathetic!
It may be to their credit . . . there's no reason to blame
Them for staying at home to avoid public shame.

The men were not there, if the theory is true,
'Cause they couldn't find anything helpful to do.
So how come the females were present that day?
Weren't the women as helpless and frightened as they?
Perhaps both were led by that social decree
That proclaims man must "act," but a woman may "be."
Those women were helpless and weak, yet they dared
To be present with Jesus . . . to show Christ they cared.
His wounds gave them pain. How they flinched at each moan!
Yet, their presence meant Jesus did not die alone!

Where Were The Men?

81

That women may "be" while the menfolk must "do"
Is turning out these days to be far from true.
That a girl must grow up as a weak, helpless lass
Is quite soundly debunked in assertiveness class.
While women achieve and find new goals to seek,
I am wondering, who will train men to be weak?
Can a man learn to weep? to admit that he's frail?
Will we ever consider this type first-class male?
Can the men stand today by the person who's died,
Or have we reached the point where we all have to hide?

There are times when I wonder just how much our souls
Have been warped by insistence on sexual roles?

Where Were The Men?

Jesus Wept

John 11:35

Some folks can learn the Psalms with ease,
Can quote Shakespeare's soliloquies,
Can sing a whole Gregorian chant;
And some folks can't.

The "cans" oft use sarcastic banter
When'ere they run across a "can't-er."
"Don't claim your memory is hazy,
Tell the truth, you're simply lazy!"

But that, dear friends, is quite unfair.
There're conscientious folk out there
Who stuff their brains with dates and facts
And find them slipping through the cracks.

Take a person I once knew;
Her name was Kathy W.
Who made a quite impassioned start
Toward learning Bible texts by heart.

Putting countless agonizing
Hours into memorizing,
Then realizing, sad but true,
A single verse was all she knew.

"The shortest verse in Holy Writ
Was written for my benefit."
Quoth Kathy, "I am not inept.
I've memorized it. (ahem) 'He wept.'"

To tell her that, in fact, the verse
Is "Jesus wept" would make it worse.
She gave it everything she had,
And one word out of two ain't bad.

The Dying Legacy

John 19:30

Legend has it, as the soul of Voltaire slipped gently
    from the realm of sound and sight,
Friends in attendance heard the philosopher
    call beseechingly for "MORE LIGHT."
Aha! Surely here is the wise one's ultimate comment
    on the ambiguity of existence, we assume,
Rather than a churlish comment on the gloominess
    of the room.
For there is something about our sense of awe
    in the presence of death
Which gives particular weight to anything uttered
    with a dying breath.
So, if one can arrange to give one's final
    worldly comments a distinguishing feature,
Why, one is practically assured of being quoted
    by an orator, or perhaps a preacher.
There are lots more sermons preached about
    Jesus' seven last words
Than there are about His thoughts concerning lilies,
    lambs, or birds.
Sooner or later every politician declaims
    the stirring cry of Nathan Hale
Shouted triumphantly just before he was summarily
    dispatched beyond the pale.
Our great ones, can we not agree,
Oft leave a dying legacy.

Time was, we only expected people who were
    especially notable
To use their final breath to say something
    particularly quotable.
But today with Hospice and all
    we've read about dying and death,

We are beginning to expect ordinary people
    to draw a profound final breath.
Chances are, at the funeral of Grampa Billy
    or Auntie Nell,
Someone will sidle up to the loved one asking,
    "Did she die well?"
And if Billy or Nell didn't take advantage
    of the death bed to make a pungent comment
    on what they believed,
Well, gosh, that's sorta embarrassing . . .
    if you are the bereaved.
How much more satisfying if the loved one can confide,
    "I'll never forget the lovely phrase mother spoke
    before she died."
And we thought living was tough! Dying is getting
    even tougher!
It's not just that we have to lie around a lot
    and suffer,
But now we've gotta watch out for our dying breath
    lest we say something stupid like,
    "Get this dang tube out of my nose"
Instead of something lovely and profound,
    deep and meaningful, like,
    "A rose is a rose is a rose!"
The pressure's intense in that final fling,
I'd rather forget the whole darn thing.

Well, forwarned is forearmed! So, I am currently engaged
    in distilling all I have learned of life and love into
    a single pithy phrase,
In preparation for my final days.
It will be embedded indelibly in my memory, ready for the
    moment I sense imminent diminution of my vital signs . . .
But, horror of horrors, what if it's like my wedding . . .
    and I forget my lines?

The Dying Legacy

As my loved ones lean closer, their hearts filled with
    remorse and regret,
They'll hear me murmer softly, "Shucks, I forget!"
Perhaps I could read my immortal words from a 3 by 5 card
    for all those mourning lads and lasses,
But chances are by then some nurse will have taken away
    my glasses.
Why, I just might come to my dying day
With nothing very uplifting to say.

When such thoughts hurl me first into a dither and then
    a pother,
I am somewhat comforted by the dying words of
    my beloved father.
As the family gathered round his bed with eager ears,
Trusting he would encapsulate the wisdom garnered in his
    many fruitful years,
These were the words my father spoke
As he rallied, just before that final stroke,
With head akimbo . . . arms akilter,
He whispered, "Change the furnace filter."
And having blessed his kin with this bon mot
Slipped down the road we all must go.

It made us sad
To lose our dad
    but
His dying words were not half bad.

The Dying Legacy

Christmas

Luke 2:1-14

WE'VE MOVED! My, that's been quite a shock!
Now, we're the new kids on the block.
We're still uncertain just which store
Contains the things we're looking for;
And wonder how the restaurants are
Or where to take our ailing car.
The unfamiliar casts a haze
Enveloping our nights and days.
Each morn some brand new task engages
Us with maps and yellow pages.

Our furniture seems out of place
Arranged in unaccustomed space.
We grope our way through life's affairs
And feel like those transplanted chairs.
For though our neighbors share advice
And really are extremely nice,
Life is not readily converted
For us, the highly introverted.
We sense 'twill take a little bit
Of time until we really fit.

We now approach The Holiday
With long-time friends so far away.
We trim these unfamiliar shelves
And feel so sorry for ourselves.
Till in our newish habitat
We turn once more to Luke and Matt.
Their words unfold a simple core
Of thoughts we've never had before.
THAT WONDROUS TALE OF STARS AND MANGERS
IS ALL ABOUT A GROUP OF STRANGERS!

Looking from our point of view
We note that family was new
To crowded, busy Bethlehem;
And now we tend to feel for them.
We see how Mary labored with-
Out support from kin or kith
And in a manger laid Christ down
'Cause Joseph didn't know the town.
(He had no prior indication
That they might need a reservation.)

Yet, God, the chief of all arrangers,
Blessed that young family of strangers.
Right in their midst God chose to dwell
And chose to be Emmanuel.
It seems in this that Heaven spoke
A special word to newish folk:
For oft we sense Amazing Grace is
Found in unfamiliar places.

We're trusting something rather pleasant
Will touch our lives this Christmas present!

Christmas